NICCI PRICE

ChatGPT Prompt Templates For Nonfiction Writers

The Only 3 ChatPGT Prompt Templates You Need To Produce Content Fast That Doesn't Suck

First edition

This book was professionally typeset on Reedsy.
Find out more at reedsy.com

Contents

Introduction

Plenty of information and books exist on using prompts in ChatGPT for improved writing. But nothing quite like this. I've engineered a few prompt templates that are usable across most nonfiction writing.

Instead of using 50 prompts or prompt sequences to get broad information and narrow it down to only one paragraph of usable content, these prompt templates shorten the amount of time spent on research, creating an outline, and drafting from days or weeks to minutes.

They also assist in the tone and style of writing you want to achieve for your nonfiction piece, making sure it relates to your reader.

Finally, the prompt templates structure the information provided by Chat-GPT in a way that is easy for you to digest and dive deeper into if you want to.

In minutes, you can have a rough outline or draft, eliminate writer's block, have accurate and credible information, have a deeper understanding of your topic, and effectively communicate its particular points to your ideal reader.

I think of ChatGPT as an assistant. To whom I was reluctant to give even the most straightforward task, like bringing me coffee. One, because I can do it myself. Two, because I can probably do it better since I already know how I like it. Three, I actually enjoy getting my own coffee. Four, I didn't want to spend time teaching an assistant.

But the more I let ChatGPT in, the more access I gave it to my processes, the better I trained it, and the more I realized how ineffective I was by not just letting it enhance and improve what I was already doing. The time and energy it saves can be focused and directed to my craft and what my job is: producing quality efficiently.

The prompt templates and process consist of two parts. First is the actual prompt template, using the words and phrases that produce the best output and response from ChatGPT. Second, is the variables you give it based on what you are writing and who you are writing it for. Both of these streamline the process considerably.

The more you use these templates, the more you'll see how proficient they are in diving deep and producing fantastic outputs using as few prompts as possible.

Here is a quick outline of the process:

1. Pertinent questions to answer about your content to ensure that you utilize the prompt templates to their fullest power.
2. Researching and gathering relevant information using the power of the prompt templates and ChatGPT.
3. Expanding the information.
4. Refining the research for the content's purpose and target audience.

Following this process ensures that ChatGPT gives responses within the context of your content with exact, descriptive, contextually relevant information in a way that is understood and readily applicable to your ideal reader or target audience to serve them best.

The process consists of 4 or 5 prompts (depending on if you're using the bonus prompt), 3 of which are prompt templates with variables.

I will use the term *content* to describe any nonfiction text or information, no matter the format. It can be a chapter within a book, a book, an article, a biography, a documentary, a speech, a script, a research paper, etc.

Initially, I will use one scenario as an example to explain how the prompt templates work. After that, I'll demonstrate the prompt templates and process by using them in various scenarios.

Pertinent Questions

ChatGPT needs to understand the context entirely to produce usable responses quickly. The quality of the output greatly depends on the quality of the input.

Without these answers, even using the templates provided, you will still only get average responses from ChatGPT.

ChatGPT is a unique trainable technology. See yourself as one of its teachers, and it will give you excellent results. Any student performs better if the teaching, training, or coaching quality is better.

How do we teach it? By answering these questions and using them in the different prompt templates. The answers to these questions are the variables you'll use in the prompt templates.

Questions to answer:

1. What is the main topic of the content?
2. Who is the ideal reader/target audience/avatar?
3. What is the purpose and tone of the content, written in what way?

Using our first scenario, these are the answers to our questions:

1. What is the main topic of the content? Building muscle.
2. Who is the ideal reader/target audience/avatar? A woman with a family looking to incorporate strength training into her daily life.
3. What is the purpose and tone of the content, written in what way? Actionable advice that she's excited to implement immediately.

Spend some time and deliberation on these questions. You may not have all three answers because you are still delving into this niche. Don't worry. The output given to us using the first three prompt templates can also help us decide which way we'd like to go.

The more you use the templates and see the outputs, the better your input variables will also become.

Researching and Gathering Information

As much as ChatGPT can help us save time, if you don't know how to use it effectively, it can quickly become laborious and an endless clicking of the "Regenerate" button. Once I got on board with the idea of working with ChatGPT, I soon ran into one of the biggest hurdles for me and other writers.

Getting information out of ChatGPT that is valid, precise, correct, and entirely relevant to a topic without needing to spend hours trying so many prompt variations that you may as well have gathered and done all the research, fact-checked every single thing that ChatGPT spits out, and structured it yourself. Especially if you know little to nothing about the topic.

The first two prompt templates allow us to get the research done so that the odds of being factually correct are high; the information is highly relevant to our topic and structured for easy readability, consumption, and understanding. The output from these prompts will also give us an outline for our content.

Prompt template #1

*Identify the top (**quantity**) authorities on (**topic**) and give me their top (**quantity**) commonly recommended advice on (**topic**). Provide it in a list.*

I know. So. Simple. But don't let its simplicity fool you. The ChatGPT response stuns and excites me every time. I've tested this template on topics I heavily researched and wrote countless words on (without using A.I.), and the accuracy is incredible. What used to take me days and weeks to research, compile,

5

outline, draft, and structure now takes me minutes.

We use authorities on our topic because it gives ChatGPT a specific data set to gather information from, i.e. all the knowledge from these authorities in our particular niche. The responses for our following prompts will be in the context of this information. With this, we further teach ChatGPT about the output we want.

It bears repeating: The better the input, the better the output.

There are three variables in this prompt template:

1. The number of authorities you'd like to use.
2. The topic of your content.
3. The number of points you want to use in your research.

I like using six or more *authorities* and *commonly recommended advice* to give ChatGPT more data to work from for the following prompts in the process. It gives more insight into the topic.

The *topic* is your answer to the first pertinent question.

For now, we want to gather the most relevant information out there, learn more about our topic, and get our creative juices flowing.

I have experimented with using different words depending on the type of nonfiction I'm writing. For example, when I'm writing a biography style or content with many facts and data, I would replace "commonly recommended advice" with "commonly shared facts and insights."

The information in the output from ChatGPT doesn't change much. It is more how the final output is written that changes. More on this later when we go through different scenarios of using the prompt templates.

The time has come for us to employ ChatGPT. Using our first scenario, our prompt is:

*Identify the top **6** authorities on **building muscle** and give me their top **6** commonly recommended advice on **building muscle**. Provide it in a list.*

ChatGPT-4 response:

While "top authorities" on building muscle can be subjective and vary over time, as of my last update in 2021, several experts are widely recognized in the fitness community for their contributions to the science and practice of muscle hypertrophy. Here are six such authorities and some commonly recommended advice from each:

1. **Arnold Schwarzenegger**
   - *Top advice:*
     1.1. Train with high volume and intensity.
     1.2. Focus on compound exercises for muscle growth (e.g., bench press, squats, deadlifts).
     1.3. Use the "mind-muscle connection" to enhance muscle activation.
     1.4. Pay attention to nutrition to support recovery and growth.
     1.5. Change up your workouts regularly to shock the muscles and avoid plateaus.
     1.6. Get adequate rest and sleep for recovery.

2. **Brad Schoenfeld, Ph.D.**
   - *Top advice:*
     2.1. Incorporate a mix of rep ranges in your training for maximum hypertrophy.
     2.2. Focus on progressive overload to continually challenge your muscles.
     2.3. Ensure adequate protein intake to support muscle protein synthesis.
     2.4. Consider periodization to optimize results over the long term.
     2.5. Pay attention to total training volume, as it's a key driver for hypertrophy.
     2.6. Rest periods should be tailored to the goal of the exercise (shorter for endurance, longer for strength).

3. **Dr. Jim Stoppani**
   - *Top advice:*
     3.1. Incorporate drop sets, supersets, and other intensity techniques.
     3.2. Make use of pre- and post-workout nutrition to fuel workouts and recovery.
     3.3. Don't neglect the importance of micronutrients and supplements.

3.4. Focus on full range of motion in exercises to maximize muscle engagement.

3.5. Include both isolation and compound movements in routines.

3.6. Listen to your body and adjust workout intensity and frequency accordingly.

4. **Dr. Stuart Phillips**

   * *Top advice:*

   4.1. Protein intake, especially post-workout, is crucial for muscle protein synthesis.

   4.2. Resistance training is the most potent stimulator of muscle protein synthesis.

   4.3. Older adults can still gain muscle, but may require more protein.

   4.4. Consistency in both training and nutrition is key.

   4.5. Aim for whole protein sources like dairy, meat, and eggs.

   4.6. Train major muscle groups at least twice a week.

5. **Louie Simmons (of Westside Barbell)**

   * *Top advice:*

   5.1. Train using the conjugate system, rotating exercises often.

   5.2. Utilize bands and chains to vary resistance and improve strength curves.

   5.3. Focus on weak points in your lifts to enhance overall strength and muscle growth.

   5.4. The importance of box squats in developing power and strength.

   5.5. Recovery modalities, like contrast showers and decompression, are important.

   5.6. Rotate between max effort and dynamic effort days.

6. **Layne Norton, Ph.D.**

   * *Top advice:*

   6.1. Train with a combination of power and hypertrophy protocols (PHAT: Power Hypertrophy Adaptive Training).

   6.2. Don't be in a prolonged caloric deficit if muscle gain is the goal.

   6.3. Nutrient timing, while not as crucial as once thought, can still be a beneficial tool.

   6.4. Overtraining is less about total volume and more about inadequate recovery.

   6.5. Consistency and adherence to a program are more critical than the "perfect" program.

   6.6. Periodize both training and nutrition for optimal results.

Remember, while these experts offer a wealth of knowledge, individual results can vary. It's crucial to listen to your own body and possibly work with a fitness professional to tailor advice to your personal circumstances.

The purpose of the next prompt in our process is to find and combine the overlapping information from these authorities, providing the subtopics of our content.

Do you see any similarities and overlaps in the advice advocated from one authority to the next? Provide them all in a list.

There are no variables in this prompt.

ChatGPT-4 response:

 Certainly, there are common themes and pieces of advice that frequently appear across different authorities in the field of muscle building. Here's a consolidated list of the overlapping advice:

1. **Importance of Compound Exercises**: Many experts emphasize the significance of compound exercises, which engage multiple muscle groups, as foundational for muscle growth (e.g., squats, deadlifts, bench press).
2. **Nutrition and Protein Intake**: The role of nutrition, particularly protein intake, in muscle recovery and growth is a recurring theme. Protein supports muscle protein synthesis, essential for hypertrophy.
3. **Progressive Overload**: Continually challenging the muscles by increasing the resistance or load over time is vital for continuous growth and strength gains.
4. **Mind-Muscle Connection**: The idea of mentally focusing on the muscle being trained to enhance muscle activation and growth.

5. **Training Volume and Intensity**: The total amount of work (sets x reps x weight) done in a workout session and the intensity of that work is key for hypertrophy. Volume is often highlighted as a primary driver for muscle growth.
6. **Consistency**: The importance of being consistent with both training and nutrition cannot be overstated. Consistent effort over time yields the best results.
7. **Recovery**: Ensuring proper rest and recovery is paramount. Overtraining or inadequate recovery can hinder progress and lead to injuries.
8. **Periodization**: Changing up workout routines or structuring training cycles to prevent plateaus and optimize long-term results.
9. **Mix of Rep Ranges**: Incorporating a variety of rep ranges in workouts can maximize hypertrophy by targeting different muscle fiber types and promoting both strength and endurance.
10. **Full Range of Motion**: Executing exercises with a full range of motion ensures maximal muscle fiber activation and growth.

11. **Listening to Your Body**: Adjusting workouts based on how one feels and understanding individual limits to prevent injuries and ensure sustainable progress.
12. **Frequency of Training**: Training major muscle groups multiple times a week can be more effective for hypertrophy than just once a week.

These recurring themes reflect foundational principles in the science and art of muscle building. While each expert may have their unique twists or specific methodologies, these core tenets are almost universally acknowledged in the field of resistance training and hypertrophy.

ChatGPT just gave us our subtopics. Now, to dive deeper.

Expanding the Information

We will expand on these points now that we have gathered relevant information from authorities. Taking into account that ChatGPT-4 has a limit to the number of characters (tokens) it can provide in its response, I go through them one by one to get as much data from a point as possible.

Prompt template #2

*For the point (**insert point**) above, in the context of (**topic**):*
   1. Give a concise explanation of what it is
   2. Explain the benefits and why it's beneficial
   3. Describe the 3 most important aspects, why they are the most important aspects of that strategy, the role of each important aspect, the process of each important aspect, the benefit of each important aspect, how each important aspect can help you achieve or implement the point
   4. Specify 3 practical pieces of advice or tips on what action to take
   5. Specify 3 practical action steps
   *6. What likely outcome(s) might there be from taking the action in the context of (**topic**)?*
   7. The key takeaway from this point.

In our second prompt template, replacing "insert point" with the first point ChatGPT gave in its previous response and "topic" with "building muscle," the third prompt and its response from ChatGPT-4 is:

*For the point **Importance of Compound Exercises** above, in the context of **Building Muscle**:*

1. *Give a concise explanation of what it is*
2. *Explain the benefits and why it's beneficial*
3. *Describe the 3 most important aspects, why they are the most important aspects of that strategy, the role of each important aspect, the process of each important aspect, the benefit of each important aspect, how each important aspect can help you achieve or implement the point*
4. *Specify 3 practical pieces of advice or tips on what action to take*
5. *Specify 3 practical action steps*
6. *What likely outcome(s) might there be from taking the action in the context of **Building Muscle**?*
7. *The key takeaway from this point.*

ChatGPT-4 response:

1. Explanation of Compound Exercises:

Compound exercises are multi-joint movements that engage multiple muscle groups simultaneously. Examples include the squat, deadlift, and bench press.

2. Benefits & Why It's Beneficial:

Benefits:

* **Efficiency**: One can target many muscles at once, leading to shorter and more productive workouts.
* **Functional Strength**: These exercises often mimic natural movement patterns, enhancing everyday functional strength.
* **Increased Muscle Activation**: Engaging multiple muscle groups leads to greater muscle fiber activation, promoting hypertrophy and strength.

3. Three Most Important Aspects:

a. **Engagement of Multiple Muscle Groups**:
- **Role**: To activate a broad spectrum of muscles during a single movement.
- **Process**: For instance, during a squat, one engages the quadriceps, hamstrings, glutes, and core.
- **Benefit**: This promotes overall muscular balance and ensures multiple muscle groups are strengthened together.

b. **Core Activation**:
- **Role**: The core stabilizes the body during compound movements.
- **Process**: When performing a deadlift, the core must contract to maintain an upright posture and protect the spine.
- **Benefit**: This simultaneous core engagement enhances overall core strength and stability, reducing the risk of injuries.

c. **Neuromuscular Coordination**:
- **Role**: To optimize movement patterns and increase the efficiency of the lift.

- **Process**: As compound exercises involve multiple joints and muscles, the nervous system must coordinate these effectively. For example, during the bench press, the chest, shoulders, and triceps work in harmony.
- **Benefit**: Improved coordination boosts athletic performance and makes everyday tasks easier.

4. Practical Pieces of Advice or Tips:

1. **Start with Proper Form**: Before adding heavy weights, ensure you're performing the movement correctly to prevent injuries.
2. **Incorporate a Mix**: Include a variety of compound movements in your routine to ensure balanced muscular development.
3. **Prioritize Compound Over Isolation**: Begin your workouts with compound exercises when you're freshest, and follow up with isolation exercises if needed.

5. Practical Action Steps:

1. **Get a Form Check**: Ask a trainer or knowledgeable gym-goer to assess your form on fundamental compound lifts.
2. **Plan a Balanced Routine**: Dedicate specific days to compound movements, e.g., a squat day, a deadlift day, and a bench press day.
3. **Progress Gradually**: Once you're comfortable with the form, slowly increase weights to challenge your muscles without risking injury.

6. Likely Outcomes in the Context of Building Muscle:

* **Enhanced Muscle Growth**: Due to increased muscle activation, one can expect accelerated hypertrophy across multiple muscle groups.
* **Improved Strength**: By engaging several muscles, compound exercises lead to more significant strength gains.
* **Balanced Physique**: Training multiple muscle groups prevents imbalances and leads to a more symmetrical and harmonious muscular development.

7. Key Takeaway:

Compound exercises are foundational for muscle building because they engage multiple muscles simultaneously, leading to efficient workouts, significant strength gains, and balanced muscle development. Prioritizing them in your routine ensures a holistic approach to strength training and hypertrophy.

The response created from this prompt is detailed. That concludes the part of the process around research.

In just three prompts, we gathered the information necessary to write our content in a clear and structured way.

Refining the Research for its Purpose and Target Audience

Understanding who our targeted audience and the purpose of our content is will bring the information we have to life. We want to convey the information to our intended reader in a way that delivers the purpose of our content. We need to make it relatable and engaging to our specific readers.

For example, let's say we just researched the topic of *Vineyards in Italy.* The piece that we are writing will look vastly different from when our audience is people who are looking to travel to the vineyards in Italy for a fun-filled vacation drinking wine, with the purpose of the information to entice them to visit.

Compared to when our audience is people who are interested in the vineyards and history of the area, and the purpose of the content is to show the reader the expansion of the vineyards and industry and how it has evolved.

Enter prompt template number three.

To illustrate the point, I will use two scenarios with our current topic of building muscle:

1. Our avatar is *a woman with a family looking to incorporate strength training into her daily life* and the purpose of our content is to *give her actionable advice that she's excited to implement.*
2. Our avatar is *a man who is underweight and looking to bulk up* and the purpose of our content is to *show him how to do it in a healthy and sustainable way.*

Again, the more specific you are here, the better the output will be.

Prompt template #3

*For the point and aspects of (**point 1**) explained above, in terms of (**topic**): Generate a comprehensive and detailed chapter. Illustrate and explain the point and aspects of that point with examples and/or anecdotes that make it more relatable to (**avatar**). Write it in a way (**purpose of content**). Use all the information provided for this point and aspects of this point in the previous responses to create in-depth and informative content.*

Scenario 1:

Prompt: *For the point and aspects of **Importance of Compound Exercises** explained above, in terms of **Building Muscle**: Generate a comprehensive and detailed chapter. Illustrate and explain the point and aspects of that point with examples and/or anecdotes that make it more relatable to **a woman with a family looking to incorporate strength training into her daily life**. Write it in a way that **gives her actionable advice that she's excited to implement**. Use all the information provided for this point and aspects of this point in the previous responses to create in-depth and informative content.*

ChatGPT-4 response:

Chapter: The Power of Compound Exercises for Modern Moms

In today's bustling world, for a woman juggling family responsibilities, career demands, and personal well-being, efficiency is key. As you're considering adding strength training to your fitness routine, you might wonder, "How can I achieve the most with limited time?" Enter the realm of compound exercises, a game-changer for women everywhere.

What are Compound Exercises?

At its core, compound exercises are multi-joint movements that engage multiple muscle groups at once. Imagine the difference between picking up a toy scattered on the floor (akin to a squat) and flexing your bicep to show off to your child. The former involves multiple muscles, while the latter focuses on just one. A squat, a deadlift, or a bench press are not just exercises; they're daily movements. Every time you lift your toddler, carry groceries, or push

Why Compound Exercises Matter for Moms

* **Efficiency**: Think of compound exercises as the ultimate multitasking tool for your muscles. Instead of isolating one muscle, you're working many at once. In the limited "me time" that you get between school runs and work deadlines, these exercises ensure you maximize every minute.
* **Functional Strength**: These exercises replicate natural movements, enhancing your functional strength. This means the strength you gain isn't just for the gym. It translates to carrying your growing child, moving furniture around for a home makeover, or lifting hefty shopping bags with ease.
* **Holistic Muscle Activation**: Compound exercises provide a well-rounded workout, ensuring you avoid imbalances. Remember the last time you felt that ache in your back after a long day? Strengthening your body holistically can help ward off such issues.

Three Key Aspects Every Mom Should Know

1. **Engaging Multiple Muscle Groups:**
    * **In Mom's Life**: Think about the times you've held your child in one arm while stirring a pot with the other. This act demands coordination from your entire body.
    * **The Benefit**: By engaging various muscles simultaneously, compound exercises promote overall balance. So, the next time you're playing tug-of-war with your kids, your arms, back, and legs are equally prepared.
2. **Core Activation:**
    * **In Mom's Life**: The core is the unsung hero when you're trying to balance a baby on one hip or when you twist to grab a rogue toy while driving.
    * **The Benefit**: Compound exercises inherently strengthen your core, enhancing posture and reducing the risk of back pain. A stronger core can also make daily chores more manageable and reduce fatigue.
3. **Neuromuscular Coordination:**
    * **In Mom's Life**: Remember the early days of motherhood when picking up your baby felt

    awkward? Over time, this became second nature because your neuromuscular coordination improved.
    * **The Benefit**: Regularly performing compound exercises improves this coordination, ensuring that you move more fluidly, whether that's during a family dance-off or an impromptu game of tag.

Mama's Action Plan: Compound Exercises

1. **Prioritize Form Over Weight**: Start with bodyweight exercises like squats or push-ups. Once you're confident in your form, consider adding weights. A simple trick? Use household items like water jugs before investing in dumbbells.
2. **Incorporate Compound Movements Daily**: Turn chores into mini workouts. Squat when picking up toys or lunge while vacuuming. Making compound movements a part of your daily routine can be fun and beneficial.
3. **Progress Gradually**: As you become more comfortable, challenge yourself. Add reps,

increase weights, or try variations. Remember, every little progress counts.

The Promise of Compound Exercises

Incorporating these exercises can lead to:

* **A Stronger You**: Not just in muscle, but in endurance. Those marathon days with back-to-back chores and kid activities? You'll power through them with added vigor.
* **A Healthier Physique**: Regular strength training, especially with compound movements, can enhance metabolism, aid in weight management, and improve bone density.
* **Boosted Confidence**: The empowerment that comes from lifting weights and feeling stronger is unparalleled. You'll not only be lifting dumbbells but also your spirits!

In Conclusion

For the modern mom, time is precious. Compound exercises respect that, offering a holistic

workout in a short span. It's not about looking like a bodybuilder; it's about building a body that can play, work, and love with strength. With every squat, press, and lift, you're not just building muscle; you're building a stronger version of yourself for the people who matter most. So, the next time you find a few minutes, remember: you have the power to compound the benefits for your body and soul.

Scenario 2:

Prompt: *For the point and aspects of* **Importance of Compound Exercises** *explained above, in terms of* **Building Muscle**: *Generate a comprehensive and detailed chapter. Illustrate and explain the point and aspects of that point with examples and/or anecdotes that make it more relatable to a* **man who is underweight and looking to bulk up***. Write it in a way that* **shows him how to do it in a healthy and sustainable way***. Use all the information provided for this point and aspects of this point in the previous responses to create in-depth and informative content.*

ChatGPT-4 response:

Chapter: Embracing Compound Exercises: The Road to a Robust You

For the slender man aspiring for a more muscular physique, the vast world of muscle-building can be both inspiring and overwhelming. You might wonder, "Where should I begin?" or "How do I ensure I'm bulking up healthily?" The cornerstone to your muscle-building journey lies in the magic of compound exercises.

Understanding Compound Exercises

At their essence, compound exercises are those that engage multiple joints and muscle groups simultaneously. Imagine these movements as the multi-taskers of the exercise world. Instead of just focusing on a singular muscle, like the biceps, compound exercises like squats, deadlifts, and bench presses pull various muscles into the action.

Why Compound Exercises are a Game-Changer for the Underweight Man

* **Efficiency**: Especially when you're starting off slender, you'd want exercises that can help you pack on muscle across multiple areas of your body without having to spend all day in the gym. Compound exercises let you do just that.
* **Functional Strength**: While aesthetic goals are valid, it's equally crucial to have real-world strength. Compound exercises translate directly to functional strength, helping you in daily activities and boosting your confidence.
* **Stable Muscle Growth**: Instead of disproportionate growth from isolation exercises, compound movements promote balanced and harmonious development.

Three Aspects Tailored to Your Bulking Journey

1. **Engaging Multiple Muscle Groups**:
    * **Relatable Scenario**: Think about when you're attempting to lift a heavy box. It's not just your arms doing the work but your legs, back, and core. This coordinated effort is the essence of compound exercises. ↻ Rege
    * **Benefit for You**: For someone underweight, this comprehensive muscle engagement

means you're not just building biceps or triceps but creating a more uniformly muscular physique.

2. **Core Activation**:
   * **Relatable Scenario**: Even simple activities, like trying to maintain balance on a moving bus or standing up straight after a long day at work, require your core.
   * **Benefit for You**: As you bulk up, a strong core ensures you maintain posture, balance, and reduce the risk of injuries. It also means that as you gain weight, you'll carry it well.
3. **Neuromuscular Coordination**:
   * **Relatable Scenario**: Remember the coordination needed when playing a sport or even video games? That precise hand-eye or foot-eye coordination has parallels in the gym.
   * **Benefit for You**: As you engage with compound exercises, you'll notice improved body coordination, leading to more effective workouts and better overall physical agility.

Your Blueprint: Incorporating Compound Exercises

1. **Prioritize Form Over Weight**: It's tempting to grab the heaviest dumbbell, but starting with the right form will set the foundation. Consider working with a trainer initially or using online resources to master the basics.
2. **Variety is Key**: Incorporate different compound exercises in your routine. While the bench press targets your chest, shoulders, and triceps, squats will focus on your lower body. A diverse routine ensures even muscle growth.
3. **Progress Gradually but Consistently**: It's essential to push your boundaries, but remember to do it safely. As you become more accustomed, increase the weight or repetitions slowly to challenge your muscles.

Anticipating the Gains

Here's what to expect as you delve into the world of compound exercises:

* **Comprehensive Muscle Growth**: With consistent effort, you'll begin to notice growth not just in isolated spots but across your entire body.
* **Improved Strength**: Everyday tasks, from lifting bags to opening jars, will become noticeably easier.

* **Enhanced Stamina and Endurance**: As you pack on muscle, you'll also find that you're less prone to getting winded or fatigued.

Concluding Thoughts

Bulking up, especially when you're starting off underweight, is a journey, not a sprint. Compound exercises provide the foundation to ensure that this journey is both efficient and holistic. You're not just aiming for a muscular appearance, but real, tangible strength that reflects in every aspect of your life. Embrace compound exercises, stay patient, and watch as your body transforms, leading you to a healthier, stronger version of yourself.

Bonus Prompt

Enhance your response by expanding on each point using examples, adding detail, more elaborate explanations and anecdotal evidence.

ChatGPT-4 bonus prompt response:

Chapter: Building A Powerful Legacy: Compound Exercises for the Aspiring Hercules

Many of us grew up with tales of Hercules and his extraordinary strength. While you may not be battling mythical beasts, if you're an underweight individual aiming to bulk up, you're fighting your own personal battles. Drawing inspiration from those stories, we can break down the Herculean task of muscle-building using compound exercises.

Diving Deep into Compound Exercises

Compound exercises are like the multi-taskers of the exercise world. Think of them as the equivalent of Hercules's Twelve Labors - each one challenging multiple parts of his being. Similarly, exercises like squats, deadlifts, and bench presses activate various muscle groups simultaneously. Imagine the squat, which doesn't merely target the legs. As you bend and rise, your thighs, glutes, core, and even back muscles spring into action, just like how Hercules used his entire body strength when he lifted and carried the heavens for Atlas.

The Herculean Benefits of Compound Exercises for Bulking Up

* **Masterful Efficiency**: Think of how Hercules had to clean the Augean stables in a single day. He couldn't focus on cleaning it bit by bit; he needed a comprehensive strategy. Similarly, compound exercises, by working on multiple muscles, help you achieve more in less time.
* **Achieving Functional Strength**: Hercules didn't just have show muscles; he used them. Likewise, compound exercises aren't just about aesthetics. They ensure you gain strength useful in real-world situations, like carrying heavy grocery bags or helping a friend move.
* **Unified Muscle Activation**: Hercules had a harmonious blend of strength and agility, ensuring he didn't face muscle imbalances. Similarly, compound exercises promote an evenly distributed muscle growth, preventing awkward imbalances and postural issues.

Three Cornerstones for Aspiring Strongmen

1. **Engaging Multiple Muscle Groups**:
    * **Example**: Reflect on Hercules wrestling the Nemean lion. It wasn't just about arm strength; he used his legs for leverage, his core for stability, and his back muscles to pull. This mirrors compound exercises, where you deploy a host of muscles to complete a move.
    * **The Benefit**: This holistic engagement means faster muscle gain. Like Hercules's multifaceted challenges, you're building diverse strengths, which amalgamate to form a bulwark of muscle and power.
2. **Core Activation**:
    * **Example**: Remember the tale where Hercules captures the Golden Hind? It wasn't raw strength but agility and balance, largely derived from a robust core. Similarly, as you deadlift, your core isn't just idling; it's stabilizing your entire body.
    * **The Benefit**: A fortified core supports everything - from lifting heavier weights without injury to maintaining posture. Over time, as Hercules learned, a strong core becomes a reservoir of inner strength, both physically and metaphorically.
3. **Neuromuscular Coordination**:
    * **Example**: Picture Hercules shooting arrows at the Stymphalian Birds. It's not just about a

keen eye or a strong arm but about the coordination between the two. As you progress with compound exercises, your body's various muscles learn to work in symphony.

* **The Benefit**: This coordination is pivotal. It ensures that as you lift, every part of your body is in sync. You'll find tasks, from lifting to throwing, become effortless, as if your muscles have rehearsed it a thousand times.

Hercules's Training Regimen: Gaining Mass the Right Way

1. **Technique Over Sheer Power**: Hercules didn't slay beasts by flailing wildly; he had technique. Begin with bodyweight exercises to master form before moving on to weights. This ensures you're laying down solid foundations.

2. **Embrace the Compound Philosophy**: Incorporate key compound exercises into every workout. Like the multifaceted challenges Hercules tackled, your muscles need diverse stimuli to grow.

3. **Evolve and Adapt**: As you progress, increase the intensity. Hercules didn't face his toughest labor first; he built up to it. Similarly, as you get stronger, challenge yourself with heavier weights and more complex movements.

The Future Forecast: A Life Transformed

Venturing into the realm of compound exercises, anticipate:

* **Visible Muscle Growth**: With time and dedication, your muscles will begin to develop, enhancing your physical appearance.
* **Surging Strength**: Tasks that once seemed daunting will become second nature as you wield the functional strength gained from compound exercises.
* **An Emanating Confidence**: As Hercules grew with each labor, you'll witness a surge in confidence. Not just in how you look, but in what you feel capable of achieving.

In Conclusion

Hercules, in his time, became a legend through his labors. While you might not be aiming for demigod status, remember that every challenge faced and conquered, every weight lifted, and every rep completed, contributes to your legacy. Compound exercises are not just a physical endeavor; they're a testament to what you can achieve. Like Hercules's Twelve Labors, think of each workout session as a step towards your monumental myth.

The bonus prompt does not necessarily generate a better response. It does, however, write it slightly differently, giving more ways of conveying the same information to the avatar.

That's our entire process.

Various Scenario Demonstrations

I will demonstrate the prompt template in different scenarios. Some of these scenarios only differ slightly to show the difference in the response, quality of the response, and the importance of knowing who you are writing for and the intended purpose of the content.

In some scenarios, for example, the biography, some points may seem unnecessary, or the wording of the prompt may sound strange. Don't overthink it. Keep in mind that these templates aim to get the best quality information that ChatGPT can provide. ChatGPT understands what you are requesting.

To keep this book concise, I will state the prompts used for each scenario but only give the final prompt's response once we've run through all the prompts for that scenario rather than the response to each prompt.

Scenario 1

Topic: Effective communication with your toddler.

Avatar: Parents or caregivers of toddlers who struggle to communicate with toddlers.

Purpose and tone of the content written in what way: Show the parents or caregivers that they are not alone in this journey. Write in a soothing, informative and entertaining way.

Prompt #1:

*Identify the top **6** authorities on **effective communication with your toddler** and give me their top **6** commonly recommended advice on **effective communication with your toddler**. Provide it in a list.*

Prompt #2:

Do you see any similarities and overlaps in the advice advocated from one authority to the next? Provide them all in a list.

Prompt #3:

*For the point **Acknowledge and Validate Emotions** above, in the context of **effective communication with your toddler**:*

1. *Give a concise explanation of what it is*
2. *Explain the benefits and why it's beneficial*
3. *Describe the 3 most important aspects, why they are the most important aspects of that strategy, the role of each important aspect, the process of each important aspect, the benefit of each important aspect, how each important aspect can help you achieve or implement the point*
4. *Specify 3 practical pieces of advice or tips on what action to take*
5. *Specify 3 practical action steps*
6. *What likely outcome(s) might there be from taking the action in the context of **effective communication with your toddler**?*
7. *The key takeaway from this point.*

Prompt #4:

*For the point and aspects of **Acknowledge and Validate Emotions** explained above, in terms of **effective communication with your toddler**: Generate a comprehensive and detailed chapter. Illustrate and explain the point and aspects of that point with examples and/or anecdotes that make it more relatable to **parents or caregivers of toddlers who struggle to communicate with toddlers**. Write it in a way that **shows the parents or caregivers that they are not alone in this journey**. **Write in a soothing, informative and entertaining way**. Use all the information provided for this point and aspects of this point in the previous responses to create* *in-depth and informative content.*

ChatGPT-4 final response:

Chapter 5: Navigating the Emotional Tides: Acknowledging and Validating Toddler Emotions

Ah, the world of toddlers! Where a missing toy can spark a storm and a blue cup instead of a red one might just bring about a monsoon. If you've ever felt bewildered, wondering how such tiny humans can harbor such vast oceans of emotion, know that you're not sailing these seas alone. Many a parent has been puzzled, trying to decode the hieroglyphics of toddler emotions. But fear not! For in this chapter, we'll unveil the compass to guide you: acknowledging and validating those very emotions.

Understanding the World Through Their Eyes

Imagine you're in a foreign country, struggling with the local language. You're desperately trying to express how hungry you are, but no one understands. Frustrating, isn't it? This is akin to a day in the life of a toddler. Their feelings are raw and genuine, but they don't always have the words to convey them. It's our role to become their interpreters.

Example: Little Amy was playing with her puzzle, trying to fit a piece for the umpteenth time. Her brows furrowed, her face turned a shade redder, and suddenly she was in tears, throwing the piece across the room. At first glance, one might think she's being naughty. But dive deeper. Amy isn't just "misbehaving"; she's expressing frustration.

The Power of Active Listening

You might think, "They're just toddlers. What could they possibly be trying to tell us with their babbling and antics?" A lot, actually! By tuning in to their cues, you're showing them that they matter.

Anecdote: Samantha, a mother of two, shared a tale of a time her son Ben was particularly grumpy after preschool. Instead of asking him to quiet down, she knelt to his level and said, "You seem upset. Did something happen at school?" To her surprise, he opened up about a toy-sharing incident. By actively listening, Samantha turned a potential tantrum into a

teachable moment.

Empathetic Responses: The Magic Balm

We've all had those days when a kind word from a loved one soothes our frazzled nerves. Toddlers are no different. Empathetic responses don't just validate their feelings, they're like verbal hugs.

Example: When toddler Jake cried because his sandwich was cut into squares instead of triangles, his dad could've dismissed it as silly. Instead, he said, "I see you wanted triangles today. That's okay, we all have our preferences." In doing so, he turned a potential meltdown into a calm conversation.

Why Avoiding Minimization is Key

Remember that time you were upset about something, shared it with someone, and they brushed it off as "not a big deal"? It felt dismissive, right? For toddlers, every emotion feels big, significant, and very real.

Anecdote: Maria recalls an evening when her daughter was inconsolable because her drawing didn't "look right." Instead of saying, "It's just a drawing," Maria acknowledged, "It's hard when things don't turn out the way we want." The result? The tears dried, and the two of them redrew the picture together.

Embarking on the Journey: Practical Steps Forward

1. **Set Aside Distractions**: Next time your toddler comes to you, teary-eyed or with a beaming smile, be present. Your emails can wait. Their emotions? Not so much.

2. **Reflect Their Emotions**: Mirroring their feelings, like saying, "You seem excited about your new toy!" makes them feel seen and understood.
3. **Offer Comfort**: A hug, a gentle touch, or even just sitting next to them can work wonders.

Charting the Course: Likely Outcomes

As you embark on this journey of acknowledging and validating, you'll notice:

* A deepening bond: Your toddler will view you as their anchor, their safe haven.
* A shift in behavior: Less confusion and more clarity, leading to fewer outbursts.
* An evolution in emotional expression: As they grow, they'll articulate their feelings better, making your job easier!

Anchoring Your Voyage: The Key Takeaway

Dear reader, as you traverse the tumultuous seas of toddlerhood, remember: Every emotion, whether it's a ripple or a tidal wave, is a cry for understanding. By acknowledging and validating, you're not just calming the storm; you're teaching them to navigate their own emotional oceans. So, hoist your sails, and know that with every gust of wind (or toddler whim!), you're becoming a more adept sailor in the vast ocean of parenting.

Note: The examples and anecdotes are fictional and crafted for illustrative purposes.   Regene

Scenario 2

Topic: Effective communication with your toddler.

Avatar: First-time parents of toddlers.

Purpose and tone of the content written in what way: Give an actionable guide written in an entertaining and informative way, using story style writing.

The first 3 prompts are the same as for scenario 1. The topic is the same as scenario 1. The avatar and purpose of the content are different.

Prompt #4:

*For the point and aspects of **Acknowledge and Validate Emotions** explained above, in terms of **effective communication with your toddler**: Generate a comprehensive and detailed chapter. Illustrate and explain the point and aspects of that point with examples and/or anecdotes that make it more relatable to **first-time parents of toddlers**. Write it in a way that **gives an actionable guide written in an entertaining and informative way, using story-style writing**. Use all the information provided for this point and aspects of this point in the previous responses to create in-depth and informative content.*

ChatGPT-4 final response:

Chapter 7: Emotions 101 – When Your Toddler's Feelings Speak Louder Than Words

Once upon a time, in a world of sticky fingers, spilled milk, and endless episodes of animated shows, Laura and Mark were first-time parents to a spirited two-year-old named Ava. Like many new parents, they had traversed the universe of sleepless nights and first steps. But now, they faced a new challenge: the tumultuous tides of toddler emotions.

Understanding the Tsunami of Emotions

Laura remembered the day Ava had a meltdown because her sandwich was cut into squares instead of triangles. "It's just a sandwich!" she thought, bewildered. But to Ava, it wasn't just about the sandwich. It was her way of saying, "I want to be heard. I have preferences."

Here's the deal. Toddlers, with their blossoming personalities and limited vocabulary, experience a whirlwind of emotions. They don't always have the words to express them, so their feelings manifest in other ways. The secret to navigating these emotional storms? Acknowledge and validate their emotions.

The Magic of Active Listening

One evening, Ava was upset because her toy was "broken" (it wasn't; she just couldn't fit the round peg into the square hole). Mark, taking a moment, sat down beside her, mimicking her focus on the toy.

"I see you're upset about the toy." he began, his voice a calm presence in Ava's stormy world. By reflecting her feelings, he made Ava feel seen and heard.

Active listening isn't about solving the problem. It's about being there, in the emotional trenches, with your child. It's a "me too" in a world that often feels big and confusing for them.

Speaking the Language of Emotion

As days went by, Laura and Mark got the hang of it. When Ava cried because her ice cream melted, instead of saying, "It's just ice cream," Laura would respond, "You're sad because your ice cream is all melty, huh?" This simple validation, repeated over time, gave Ava a vocabulary for her emotions. She started using words, saying things like "I'm mad!" instead of tossing toys.

Every time they reflected her emotions back at her, it was like they were giving her a little piece of the emotional puzzle, helping her make sense of her feelings.

Creating a Judgment-Free Zone

One sunny afternoon, at a playdate, Ava took a toy from another child. Embarrassed, Laura's initial reaction was to scold. But recalling the principle of a non-judgmental response, she took a deep breath.

"I see you wanted that toy. It's hard to wait your turn, isn't it?" Laura acknowledged. By doing this, she wasn't condoning the behavior. Instead, she was creating an environment where Ava could learn from the situation without feeling shamed.

Tales from Other Guardians of Toddlers

Every parent, at some point, feels they're on a lonely island, battling the wild seas of toddlerhood alone. But guess what? Laura and Mark soon realized they weren't the only sailors on this voyage.

Sarah, their neighbor, once laughed about how her three-year-old cried because he couldn't wear swimming goggles to bed. And Raj from the local playground spoke of how his daughter wailed because her banana broke in half.

Toddlers everywhere, with their wonderfully illogical reasons, just yearn to be understood.

Your Actionable Guide

1. **Join their world**: Next time there's a tantrum brewing, instead of towering above, get down to their eye level. See the world from their perspective.
2. **Become a parrot (sort of)**: Reflect their emotions in simple language. "You're sad about the banana?" might sound repetitive to you, but for them, it's comforting validation.
3. **Avoid the "fix-it" urge**: Sometimes, they don't want solutions. They just want a listening ear.

What's Beyond the Horizon?

By acknowledging and validating, not only will the stormy seas become a tad calmer, but you're also laying the foundation for open communication in the future. Your little one will come to know that they can always talk to you, no matter how big or small their feelings are.

Final Nautical Note

Remember, dear sailor, while the tides of toddler emotions might seem overwhelming, with every acknowledgment and validation, you're steering your ship closer to the shores of understanding and trust. The voyage is long, but oh, the treasures you'll discover along the way!

Scenario 3

Topic: The shortest path to financial success
   Avatar: Entrepreneurs and small business owners
   Purpose of the content: Giving an actionable guide.

Prompt #1:
   *Identify the top 6 authorities on **the shortest path to financial success** and give me their top 6 commonly recommended advice on **the shortest path to financial success**. Provide it in a list.*

Prompt #2:

Do you see any similarities and overlaps in the advice advocated from one authority to the next? Provide them all in a list.

Prompt #3:

*For the point **Invest for the Long Term** above, in the context of **the shortest path to financial success**:*

1. *Give a concise explanation of what it is*
2. *Explain the benefits and why it's beneficial*
3. *Describe the 3 most important aspects, why they are the most important aspects of that strategy, the role of each important aspect, the process of each important aspect, the benefit of each important aspect, how each important aspect can help you achieve or implement the point*
4. *Specify 3 practical pieces of advice or tips on what action to take*
5. *Specify 3 practical action steps*
6. *What likely outcome(s) might there be from taking the action in the context of **the shortest path to financial success**?*
7. *The key takeaway from this point.*

Prompt #4:

*For the point and aspects of **Invest for the Long Term** explained above, in terms of **the shortest path to financial success**: Generate a comprehensive and detailed chapter. Illustrate and explain the point and aspects of that point with examples and/or anecdotes that make it more relatable to **Entrepreneurs and small business owners**. Write it in a way that **gives an actionable guide**. Use all the information provided for this point and aspects of this point in the previous responses to create in-depth and informative content.*

ChatGPT-4 final response:

Chapter: The Long Game - Investing for Entrepreneurs and Small Business Owners

Entrepreneurs and small business owners often find themselves on a thrilling roller coaster of financial ups and downs. As they navigate their businesses' challenges and successes, there's an underlying strategy that could significantly amplify their financial success: Investing for the long term. By understanding and harnessing this principle, entrepreneurs can create a robust financial future for themselves, even beyond their businesses.

The Essence of Long-Term Investing

At its core, investing for the long term involves strategically placing money in investments and allowing them to grow over extended periods. Instead of reacting to short-term market fluctuations, this strategy focuses on the bigger picture.

Example: Imagine an entrepreneur, Alex, who began investing a portion of his business profits in a diverse portfolio. The first year, the market was rocky, but instead of withdrawing or halting his investments due to fear, Alex persisted. Fast forward 20 years, those early investments, compounded with his consistent contributions, have grown into a substantial nest egg, providing him both security and flexibility in his entrepreneurial endeavors.

Diversification: Spreading Your Bets

Every entrepreneur understands the risk. Just as they diversify their business offerings to mitigate risks, diversifying their investment portfolio can help shield them from adverse market events.

Anecdote: Sara, a successful boutique owner, once faced a significant business downturn when a new competitor emerged. Instead of banking solely on her shop's success, she had diversified her investments across stocks, real estate, and bonds. So, while her business faced challenges, her personal finances remained resilient, allowing her to strategize and rebound without the pressure of financial distress.

Actionable Guide: As an entrepreneur, start by setting aside a percentage of your profits for investment. Distribute these funds across different asset classes, industries, and possibly even countries. This approach not only hedges against risk but can also unlock various growth opportunities.

Regular Contributions: The Power of Consistency

Dollar-cost averaging, a fancy term for making regular contributions, can be an entrepreneur's best friend. By investing consistent amounts at regular intervals, you can benefit from market lows and highs alike.

Example: Consider Mike, who owns a thriving digital agency. He sets up an automated system to invest a fixed sum every month. When the market dips, his consistent contributions buy more shares, and during peaks, he gains from the increased value. Over time, Mike enjoys a healthy average return without the stress of timing the market.

Actionable Guide: Entrepreneurs can set up automated transfers from their business accounts to their investment accounts. This "set it and forget it" approach ensures consistent investment, compounding their potential returns.

Continuous Review and Rebalancing: The Entrepreneurial Pivot

Just as businesses occasionally need to pivot based on market demand, investment portfolios require periodic reviews and adjustments.

Anecdote: Recall Lisa, who started a catering business. Over time, she noticed a growing demand for vegan options and adjusted her offerings accordingly. Similarly, after her yearly portfolio review, she noticed some stocks outperforming others, causing an imbalance. By reallocating her assets, she maintained her desired risk-reward ratio, optimizing her returns.

Actionable Guide: Entrepreneurs should treat their investments like a vital branch of their business. Schedule regular check-ins, at least annually, to assess performance. If an asset class is over or underperforming, adjust the allocation to match your original strategy and risk tolerance.

Practical Wisdom for Entrepreneurs:

1. **Stay Patient:** Just as businesses don't boom overnight, investments need time. Resist the urge to panic during market downturns.

2. **Educate Yourself:** Dive into investment knowledge as you would with industry trends. The more informed you are, the better your decisions.
3. **Seek Expertise:** Engage with financial advisors or investment mentors, just as you'd seek mentorship in business.

Tangible Steps Forward:

1. **Automate Investments:** Use digital platforms or banking tools that support automatic transfers to investment accounts.
2. **Craft a Diverse Portfolio:** Explore various investment options. Don't put all your eggs in one basket.
3. **Commit to Regular Reviews:** Mark your calendar for periodic portfolio check-ins. Stay involved.

The Bright Horizon Ahead

For entrepreneurs walking the path to financial success, long-term investing isn't just a strategy; it's a mindset. It promises consistent wealth accumulation, shielding from short-term business setbacks, and potentially opens doors to financial independence.

In essence, by committing to the long game, you're not just building a business but a legacy.

Key Takeaway: The entrepreneurial journey is filled with unpredictabilities. Investing for the long term provides a stable foundation, turning the unpredictable into a calculated strategy for success. Whether your business soars or faces challenges, a well-structured investment approach ensures your financial growth remains uninterrupted.

Scenario 4

Topic: The shortest path to financial success

Avatar: Entrepreneurs and small business owners with financial constraints

Purpose of the content: Giving an actionable guide.

The first 3 prompts are the same as for scenario 3. The topic and purpose of the content are the same as in scenario 3. The avatar is different.

Prompt #4:

*For the point and aspects of **Invest for the Long Term** explained above, in terms of **the shortest path to financial success**: Generate a comprehensive and detailed chapter. Illustrate and explain the point and aspects of that point with examples and/or anecdotes that make it more relatable to **Entrepreneurs and small business owners with financial constraints**. Write it in a way that **gives an actionable guide**. Use all the information provided for this point and aspects of this point in the previous responses to create in-depth and informative content.*

ChatGPT-4 final response:

Chapter: Navigating Financial Constraints: Long-Term Investing for Entrepreneurs on a Budget

Entrepreneurship often comes with financial constraints, especially during the early phases. However, even with limited resources, there's an overarching strategy that can set the foundation for lasting financial success: Investing for the long term. Entrepreneurs can leverage this principle, irrespective of budget limitations, to build a promising financial future.

The Core of Long-Term Investing

Long-term investing is about having a future-focused vision. It entails putting your money

into investments and letting them compound over time, resisting the urge to make hasty decisions based on transient market events.

Example: Think of Carla, an entrepreneur running a small cafe. With tight margins, she could only spare a tiny portion of her income for investments. But she started early, and over two decades, even her modest contributions compounded into a sizeable fund, giving her a financial safety net.

Diversification: Smart Choices on a Budget

For cash-strapped entrepreneurs, every penny counts. Diversifying your investments ensures that you're not overly reliant on one asset, offering a buffer against unexpected downturns.

Anecdote: Sam, who launched a shoe-repair shop, had limited funds. Instead of pouring all his savings into high-risk stocks hoping for a quick win, he spread his limited investment across various assets. When a market downturn affected one segment, his other investments cushioned the blow.

Actionable Guide: Even if you're starting small, explore micro-investing platforms. These allow you to invest minimal amounts across a range of assets, enabling diversification without demanding a hefty initial sum.

Regular Contributions: Maximizing Minimal

Even on a tight budget, consistent and regular contributions can work wonders over time. This approach can lessen the sting of market lows and highs.

Example: Ravi, who ran a budget IT consultancy, wasn't making huge profits. However, he committed to investing a small, fixed sum from every project. Over time, these small contributions, made consistently, yielded returns that far outstripped their humble origins.

Actionable Guide: Prioritize investments as you would any essential business expense. No matter how small the amount, maintain the discipline to contribute consistently. Over time, the magic of compounding will amplify these contributions.

Continuous Review and Rebalancing: Keeping Pace with Limited Resources

With limited resources, it's crucial to ensure that every dollar is working effectively. Periodically reviewing and rebalancing your portfolio keeps it aligned with your financial goals.

Anecdote: Lina, with her small online store, couldn't afford a financial advisor. Still, she dedicated a day each year to review her investments. This self-taught discipline ensured that her limited funds were always allocated in the most promising sectors.

Actionable Guide: Make use of free online tools and resources to track and evaluate your investments. Regularly review your portfolio's performance and, if necessary, adjust your allocations to ensure it aligns with your long-term goals.

Practical Wisdom for Entrepreneurs with Financial Constraints:

1. **Be Resourceful:** There are many free resources online, from blogs to webinars, that can help guide your investment journey. Knowledge is power (and profit)!
2. **Stay Consistent:** Whether it's $10 or $100, the key is consistency. Over time, your

contributions will compound and grow.
3. **Limit Fees:** Especially when starting small, look for investment platforms with minimal fees. Over time, these fees can eat into your returns.

Tangible Steps Forward:

1. **Start Now, However Small:** Begin with whatever amount you can spare. Consistency trumps the initial amount.
2. **Leverage Micro-Investing Platforms:** These platforms allow you to invest with minimal amounts, making it easier to start your journey.
3. **Educate Yourself:** Dedicate some time each week to learn more about investment basics. This will empower you to make informed decisions, even on a budget.

The Horizon Beyond the Constraints

Financial constraints don't have to stifle your journey to wealth. By focusing on the long term, even entrepreneurs on a strict budget can pave their way to financial stability and success.

In essence, long-term investing offers the hope that, even with humble beginnings, the end can be prosperous.

Key Takeaway: Long-term investing is not just for the wealthy. It's a strategy, a mindset, and a commitment. Entrepreneurs, irrespective of their current financial status, can leverage this approach to build a financially secure future. It's about starting where you are, with what you have, and keeping an eye on the long game.

Scenario 5

Topic: The shortest path to financial success

Avatar: Entrepreneurs and small business owners who are struggling with customer acquisition.

Purpose of the content: Giving an actionable guide.

The first 3 prompts are the same as for scenario 3. The topic and purpose of the content are the same as in scenarios 3 and 4. The avatar is different.

Prompt #4:

*For the point and aspects of **Invest for the Long Term** explained above, in terms of **the shortest path to financial success**: Generate a comprehensive and detailed chapter. Illustrate and explain the point and aspects of that point with examples and/or anecdotes that make it more relatable to **Entrepreneurs and small business owners who are struggling with customer acquisition**. Write it in a way that **gives an actionable guide.** Use all the information provided for this point and aspects of this point in the previous responses to create in-depth and informative content.*

ChatGPT-4 final response:

Chapter: Playing the Long Game: How Long-Term Investing Complements Customer Acquisition Struggles

Entrepreneurs and small business owners face multifaceted challenges, with customer acquisition often being the most daunting. But as you navigate the maze of attracting customers, there's a parallel financial strategy to consider: Investing for the long term. Just as customer relationships take time to foster, your finances can benefit from a long-haul perspective, providing a cushion against current operational struggles.

Grasping Long-Term Investing Amidst Customer Acquisition Struggles

Long-term investing emphasizes the significance of looking ahead, much like customer acquisition. It's about setting aside funds, irrespective of the amount, and letting them grow over time, insulating yourself from immediate market tremors.

Example: Meet Clara, who started a niche e-commerce store. While she struggled to attract an audience in the saturated online marketplace, she made it a point to invest a small fraction of her initial capital. This amount, over the years, grew and provided her with additional resources to revamp her marketing, ultimately improving her customer base.

Diversification: Broadening Horizons Beyond Business Operations

While you're focusing on multiple marketing channels to reach your audience, it's equally beneficial to diversify where your money is parked.

Anecdote: John, with his fledgling app development firm, found it challenging to land consistent clients. While grappling with this, he diversified his investments into stocks, bonds, and even a bit into cryptocurrency. When the crypto unexpectedly surged, John had the extra funds to launch a targeted ad campaign, which significantly boosted his client acquisition.

Actionable Guide: Treat your investments as you would your marketing channels. Don't rely solely on one; diversify to enhance stability and potential growth.

Regular Contributions: Building Steadily Amidst Challenges

Similar to how consistent marketing can gradually build brand recognition, regular

contributions to your investments, however minor, can pay off over the long run.

Example: Naomi, operating a small local bakery, faced stiff competition. Her regular customer base was limited. Despite these struggles, Naomi consistently allocated a tiny percentage of her monthly income to investments. Over time, this allowed her to finance a successful loyalty program, enhancing repeat business.

Actionable Guide: Determine a fixed, manageable percentage of your business revenue as your investment. Irrespective of your customer acquisition rates, ensure this sum is consistently directed towards your long-term financial goals.

Continuous Review and Rebalancing: The Investment-Marketing Analogy

Marketing strategies require tweaks based on performance metrics. Similarly, long-term investments need periodic reviews to ensure they align with financial goals.

Anecdote: Roberto's startup focused on selling sustainable goods. Despite having a worthy cause, attracting a stable customer base was tough. While refining his marketing approach, Roberto also rebalanced his investment portfolio, shifting from underperforming assets to more promising ones, providing him the financial leeway to experiment with different customer acquisition strategies.

Actionable Guide: Make it a ritual to periodically evaluate both your marketing strategies and your investment portfolio. Adjusting based on performance in both areas ensures optimized returns and growth.

Practical Wisdom for Entrepreneurs Facing Acquisition Struggles:

1. **Consistent Messaging and Investing:** Just as maintaining a consistent brand voice attracts customers, consistent investment practices compound growth.
2. **Stay Informed:** Keep abreast of both marketing trends and investment landscapes. Tools, techniques, and opportunities evolve, and staying updated can provide an edge.
3. **Financial Cushion:** Your investments can serve as a financial cushion, providing funds to experiment with new customer acquisition strategies or even pivot your business if needed.

Tangible Steps Forward:

1. **Begin with Research:** Identify low-cost, diversified investment opportunities suitable for

your financial standing.

2. **Automation:** Use automated platforms to consistently allocate a portion of your income to investments.

3. **Engage with a Mentor or Advisor:** Just as you'd seek guidance for marketing, consider consulting a financial advisor, even if it's just a one-off session to set direction.

Balancing Immediate Concerns with Long-Term Visions

In entrepreneurship, the road to acquiring a loyal customer base can be long and winding. However, parallely building a solid financial foundation through long-term investments ensures that while you're working on present challenges, your future is secure.

Key Takeaway: Long-term investing, akin to customer acquisition, is a testament to patience, persistence, and adaptability. For entrepreneurs navigating the turbulent waters of acquiring customers, having a long-term financial strategy can act as the anchor, stabilizing the journey and ensuring sustainable growth.

Scenario 6

Topic: Vineyards in Italy

Avatar: Someone traveling to the vineyards in Italy for a fun-filled vacation, drinking and learning about wine.

Purpose of the content: Entice them to visit.

Prompt #1:

*Identify the top 6 authorities on **the vineyards in Italy** and give me their top 6 commonly shared facts and insights about **the vineyards in Italy**. Provide it in a list.*

Here, you can change the template's wording from "commonly recommended advice" to "commonly shared facts and insights." As previously mentioned, the information provided by ChatGPT doesn't necessarily change. How it is written by ChatGPT changes.

Prompt #2:

Do you see any similarities and overlaps in the advice advocated from one authority to the next? Provide them all in a list.

Prompt #3:

*For the point **Wine and Food Pairing** above, in the context of **the vineyards in Italy**:*

1. *Give a concise explanation of what it is*
2. *Explain the benefits and why it's beneficial*
3. *Describe the 3 most important aspects, why they are the most important aspects of that strategy, the role of each important aspect, the process of each important aspect, the benefit of each important aspect, how each important aspect can help you achieve or implement the point*
4. *Specify 3 practical pieces of advice or tips on what action to take*
5. *Specify 3 practical action steps*
6. *What likely outcome(s) might there be from taking the action in the context of **the vineyards in Italy**?*
7. *The key takeaway from this point.*

Prompt #4:

*For the point and aspects of **Wine and Food Pairing** explained above, in terms of **the vineyards in Italy**: Generate a comprehensive and detailed chapter. Illustrate and explain the point and aspects of that point with examples and/or anecdotes that make it more relatable to **Someone traveling to the vineyards in Italy for a fun-filled vacation, drinking and learning about wine**. Write it in a way that **Entices them to visit**. Use all the information provided for this point and aspects of this point in the previous responses to create in-depth and informative content.*

ChatGPT-4 final response:

Chapter 5: The Art of Italian Wine and Food Pairing

Imagine you're nestled among the rolling hills of Tuscany, seated at a long wooden table adorned with olives, cheeses, and rustic bread. A glass of ruby-red Chianti stands before you, its aroma promising a world of flavor. As you sip, a plate of tomato-rich spaghetti all'aglione is placed in front of you. The first bite paired with the wine is not just a culinary experience—it's a symphony.

Welcome to the art of wine and food pairing, Italian-style.

Wine and Food: The Italian Love Story

In Italy, wine isn't just a drink; it's an integral part of culture, history, and everyday life. Each bottle tells a story of the land, the weather, and the people who made it. And what's a good

story without a perfect companion? Enter Italian cuisine. Together, they create magic. When wine and food dance harmoniously, they elevate each other to unprecedented levels, transforming a simple meal into an unforgettable journey.

Example: Consider Prosecco, Italy's famed sparkling wine from Veneto. On a fun-filled vacation, you might find yourself in Valdobbiadene, the heartland of Prosecco. Here, Prosecco isn't just a bubbly drink; it's a celebration of life. Paired with local cicchetti, or small snacks, like creamy codfish spread on polenta or stuffed olives, you're not just tasting wine and food—you're tasting centuries of tradition.

The Guiding Principles of Pairing

The essence of wine and food pairing lies in three cardinal principles.

1. **Flavor Balance:**

* Balance is the foundation of pairing. A robust red like Barolo from Piedmont might overpower a delicate bruschetta but will shine with a rich truffle risotto.

Anecdote: On a trip to Alba, the truffle capital, imagine being served a plate of this risotto, earthy and fragrant. Paired with Barolo, it feels like they were made for each other, each bite and sip complementing and amplifying the other.

1. **Matching Components**:

* This is the art of aligning the elements of wine and food. A tangy Frascati from Lazio, with its zesty acidity, works wonders with a fresh Caesar salad.

Example: Picture yourself in a sunlit Roman trattoria, savoring artichokes alla Romana, a Roman delicacy. A sip of Frascati, and the artichokes' richness is beautifully cut through,

making for a delightful experience.

1. **Local Pairings**:

* When in Italy, do as the Italians do. Relish the wines with local dishes. Sicily's Nero d'Avola with a hearty caponata is an islander's dream.

Anecdote: Imagine traveling down the picturesque lanes of Sicily, with its sun-drenched beaches and vibrant markets. Stumbling upon a local eatery, you're served caponata, an aubergine delight. A glass of Nero d'Avola on the side, and suddenly, every flavor is heightened, each bite more memorable than the last.

Making the Most of Your Vineyard Vacation

1. **Become a Student**: Attend pairing workshops at vineyards. Let the vintners guide you. Their

tales, interwoven with wisdom and passion, will make the wines come alive.

2. **Ask the Locals:** Don't shy away from asking for recommendations. More often than not, you'll discover hidden gems not listed in guidebooks.

3. **Experiment:** Italy offers a plethora of wines and dishes. Mix and match. Create your own pairings. Remember, there's no right or wrong, just what delights your palate.

The Promise of Italy

Your journey through Italy's vineyards promises more than just wine; it promises experiences. The joy of sipping a crisp Soave while gazing at the Veneto plains or relishing a bold Amarone with Osso Buco in a Veronese villa is unparalleled. With every pairing, you unlock a piece of Italy's soul, wrapped in centuries of tradition and love.

Key Takeaway: Italy beckons with its wines and cuisines, each telling a tale of the land and its people. Embrace the art of pairing, and you won't just be tasting—you'll be embarking on a journey through time, culture, and passion. So, pack your bags and let Italy's vineyards serenade you with their symphony of flavors.

Scenario 7

Topic: Vineyards in Italy

Avatar: Someone who is interested in the vineyards and history of the area.

Purpose of the content: Show the expansion of the vineyards and industry and how it has evolved over time.

The first 3 prompts are the same as for scenario 6. The topic is the same as in scenario 6. The avatar and purpose of the content are different.

Prompt #4:

*For the point and aspects of **Wine and Food Pairing** explained above, in terms of **the vineyards in Italy**: Generate a comprehensive and detailed chapter. Illustrate and explain the point and aspects of that point with examples and/or anecdotes that make it more relatable to **Someone who is interested in the vineyards and history of the area**. Write it in a way that **Shows the expansion of the vineyards and industry and how it has evolved over time**. Use all the information provided for this point and aspects of this point in the previous responses to create in-depth and informative content.*

ChatGPT-4 final response:

Chapter 5: Wine and Food Pairing: A Journey Through Italy's Vinicultural Legacy

Amidst the sprawling landscapes of Italy, where ancient ruins merge with modern life, lies a story as old as time: the evolution of Italian wine and its inseparable bond with food. The vineyards, more than just plots of land, are living chronicles that have witnessed the rise and fall of empires, the blending of cultures, and the passion of generations.

The Deep Roots of Italy's Wine Legacy

Long before Italy became a hub for tourists, its fertile soil was the cradle of viticulture. The Etruscans, then the Romans, cultivated vines, intertwining wine's essence with Italy's very identity. With the expansion of the Roman Empire, vines were planted far and wide, laying the foundation of what would become one of the world's premier wine regions.

Anecdote: Ancient Roman texts often spoke of *convivium*, a gathering centered around food and wine. Imagine a banquet in Pompeii, where dishes like roasted dormouse were enjoyed with wines stored in amphorae, setting early precedents for the art of pairing.

Guiding Principles of Pairing: A Historical Perspective

As the vineyards expanded, so did the understanding of wine's relationship with food:

1. **Flavor Balance:**

* From the Renaissance feasts to today's osterias, the balance has always been key. Over time, as culinary arts evolved, so did the wines, each influencing the other.

Example: In the medieval times of Tuscany, a knight returning from the Crusades might have brought exotic spices that influenced local cuisine. With the introduction of these new flavors, winemakers too adapted, producing wines that could stand up to these richer tastes.

1. **Matching Components:**

* The understanding of matching wine components with food grew as trade flourished. As new ingredients found their way to Italian shores, the wines too evolved in complexity.

  Anecdote: Venice, a hub of the spice trade, saw an influx of ingredients like black pepper and cinnamon. This demanded wines with greater depth and structure. It was during such times that wines like Valpolicella began to gain prominence, able to complement the evolving Venetian cuisine.

1. **Local Pairings:**

* The concept of 'terroir'—the idea that the land's unique characteristics influence the flavor of wine—has ancient roots. As different regions of Italy developed their culinary identities, so did their wines.

  Example: The coastal region of Liguria, with its abundant olive groves and seafood, birthed the crisp Vermentino. This wine, with its minerality and hints of citrus, was a reflection of the Mediterranean breeze and paired exquisitely with the region's fresh produce.

The Evolution of the Vineyards

Over the centuries, as wars raged and empires crumbled, the vineyards stood resilient. They became symbols of hope, continuity, and Italian pride. The post-Roman era saw the monasteries preserving and enhancing viticultural techniques. By the Middle Ages, regions like Piedmont and Lombardy emerged as viticultural centers.

The Renaissance ushered in an era of exploration and refinement. As the world was 'rediscovered', so were ancient wine-making techniques. The vineyards expanded, both in size and variety.

The 20th century, marked by industrialization and globalization, brought challenges and opportunities. While two World Wars threatened the vineyards, the periods of peace that followed saw immense growth and technological advancements.

Legacy in a Bottle

Today, as you walk through any Italian vineyard, from the terraced landscapes of Cinque Terre to the volcanic soils of Sicily, remember: every bottle is a journey through time. With every sip, you're not just tasting wine; you're experiencing a fragment of Italy's history.

Key Takeaway: Italy's wine and its pairing with food is more than a culinary endeavor. It's a testament to resilience, adaptation, and passion. The vineyards, with their deep roots, are not just sources of world-class wine but also guardians of Italy's rich legacy. For someone keen on history, every vineyard visit and every paired meal is a step closer to understanding Italy's soul.

Scenario 8

Topic: Kobe Bryant

Avatar: Someone who aspires to become the next Kobe Bryant.

Purpose and tone of the content written in what way: Biographical, informative, entertaining, and inspirational with ways to implement in their own life.

Prompt #1:

*Identify the top **6** authorities on **Kobe Bryant** and give me their top **6** commonly shared facts and insights about **Kobe Bryant**. Provide it in a list.*

Prompt #2:

Do you see any similarities and overlaps in the advice advocated from one authority to the next? Provide them all in a list.

Prompt #3:

*For the point **Team Dynamics** above, in the context of **Kobe Bryant**:*

1. *Give a concise explanation of what it is*

2. *Explain the benefits and why it's beneficial*

3. *Describe the 3 most important aspects, why they are the most important aspects of that strategy, the role of each important aspect, the process of each important aspect, the benefit of each important aspect, how each important aspect can help you achieve or implement the point*

4. *Specify 3 practical pieces of advice or tips on what action to take*

5. *Specify 3 practical action steps*

6. *What likely outcome(s) might there be from taking the action in the context of* **Kobe Bryant***?*

7. *The key takeaway from this point.*

Prompt #4:

For the point and aspects of **Team Dynamics** *explained above, in terms of* **Kobe Bryant***: Generate a comprehensive and detailed chapter. Illustrate and explain the point and aspects of that point with examples and/or anecdotes that make it more relatable to* **Someone who aspires to become the next Kobe Bryant***. Write it in a way that is* **Biographical, informative, entertaining, and inspirational with ways to implement in their own life***. Use all the information provided for this point and aspects of this point in the previous responses to create in-depth and informative content.*

ChatGPT-4 final response:

Chapter 7: Mastering the Dance of Team Dynamics - Kobe Bryant's Symphony of Success

The spotlight often gleams brightest on a singular talent, and in the realm of basketball, few shone as luminously as Kobe Bryant. Yet, behind the dunks, the fadeaways, and the game-winners, there lay a narrative far richer than the tale of one man. It's the story of a team and its intricate dance of dynamics.

To the aspiring basketball prodigy aiming to become the next 'Black Mamba,' there's an essential lesson: mastering the team's inner workings is as vital as any individual skill. Let's take a journey into the heart of Kobe's Lakers, revealing the nuanced layers of team dynamics.

Communication: The Lifeline of Legends

If basketball were a symphony, communication would be its conductor. For Bryant, it wasn't just about speaking; it was about speaking right. Remember the 2009 playoffs? In a heated

moment, Kobe calmly directed Pau Gasol during a timeout. This wasn't an angry superstar lashing out but a leader guiding his teammate. They communicated, recalibrated, and clinched the game.

To the Next Kobe: Begin with active listening. Understand before seeking to be understood. Practice clear communication during training sessions. It's more than calling plays; it's about building a bridge of understanding.

Trust: The Glue of the Greats

Who can forget the iconic alley-oop from Kobe to Shaq during the 2000 Western Conference Finals? That single play was a crystalline example of trust. Despite their notorious differences off the court, in that moment of play, they relied on each other implicitly. Their trust was their strength.

To the Next Kobe: Trust is built over time. It's about consistent actions, not grand gestures. Engage in off-the-court activities with your teammates. Get to know them beyond the game.

A simple coffee or a shared workout can forge bonds that shine during game-time.

Leadership and Role Definition: The Orchestra's Maestro

Kobe wasn't born a leader; he evolved into one. Early in his career, he played alongside giants like Shaq. As he matured, he embraced leadership, guiding the Lakers through their successes and failures. A pivotal moment illustrating this was in the 2008 Olympics, where Kobe, amidst an array of superstars, assumed a role that wasn't just about scoring but about leading and motivating.

To the Next Kobe: Recognize that roles aren't static. They evolve as you evolve. Embrace mentorship, both as a mentee and a mentor. Learning from seasoned players will give you wisdom, while guiding younger ones will refine your leadership.

Incorporating Team Dynamics into Your Game

1. **Engage in Team-Building:** This doesn't mean clichéd trust falls. Organize outings, movie nights, or even shared charity work. Strengthen the personal ties that translate into on-court chemistry.
2. **Open Forums:** Create a safe space for teammates to voice concerns, discuss strategies, or even share personal challenges. This can be during team meetings or dedicated sessions.
3. **Embrace Mentorship:** Reach out to seasoned players. Ask them about team dynamics, how they handled conflicts, and how they built trust.

Expected Outcomes: Improved understanding among team members, enhanced on-field performance, and a camaraderie that opponents will envy. As seen with Kobe and the Lakers, strong team dynamics can lead to championship victories and create a legacy of resilience.

Key Takeaway

While the world saw the fadeaways, the 81-point game, and the five championships, the real magic was often in the huddles, the training sessions, and the locker room chats. Kobe Bryant's legacy is not just a tale of individual greatness but a testament to the power of team dynamics.

To the aspiring Kobe out there, remember: Your team isn't behind you; they're beside you. Embrace them, nurture the dynamics, and together, craft a legacy that resonates through the ages.

Scenario 9

Topic: Kobe Bryant

Avatar: Someone who wants to learn more about Kobe Bryant, his achievements, and how he became successful.

Purpose and tone of the content written in what way: Documentary style, entertaining, and inspirational.

The first 3 prompts are the same as for scenario 8. The topic is the same as in scenario 8. The avatar and purpose of the content are different.

Prompt #4:

For the point and aspects of **Team Dynamics** *explained above, in terms of* **Kobe Bryant***: Generate a comprehensive and detailed chapter. Illustrate and explain the point and aspects of that point with examples and/or anecdotes that make it more relatable to* **Someone who wants to learn more about Kobe Bryant, his achievements, and how he became successful.** *Write it in a* **Documentary style, entertaining, and inspirational.** *Use all the information provided for this point and aspects of this point in the previous responses to create in-depth and informative content.*

ChatGPT-4 final response:

Chapter 7: The Symphony of the Mamba: The Unseen Team Dynamics Behind Kobe Bryant's Stardom

Fade in: A misty morning at the Lakers' practice facility. As the sun's first rays pierce through, Kobe Bryant is already in the midst of a grueling practice session. But as the camera zooms out, it's evident he's not alone. The entire Lakers team, though blurry in the backdrop, is moving in unison.

Narrator: "While Kobe Bryant's name stands tall in the annals of basketball history, the secret harmony behind the Lakers' success was an orchestra of intricate team dynamics."

The Art of Communication: The Echo of the Mamba

Cut to: Footage of a Lakers' game, where Kobe gestures animatedly, guiding his teammates.

Narrator: "Every championship team has a heartbeat, and for the Lakers, it was communication. It was the bridge between Kobe and his teammates."

Flashback: The 2009 playoffs. A crunch moment. Kobe is seen talking to Pau Gasol, not with anger, but with precision. Gasol nods, they execute, and the Lakers gain a critical edge.

Derek Fisher (Ex-teammate, in an interview setting): "Kobe didn't just talk. He communicated. There's a difference. It was strategic, timed, and always about the bigger picture."

Trust: Beyond the Shadows and the Spotlight

Clip: The iconic alley-oop from Kobe to Shaq in the 2000 Western Conference Finals.

Narrator: "Trust. An invisible thread that bound Kobe to his team. For every solo highlight reel, there were countless unseen moments of reliance."

Jeanie Buss (Lakers' owner): "They had differences. Kobe and Shaq were like fire and ice off the court. But on it? Pure synchrony. That's trust."

Leadership & Role Definition: The Evolution of a Maestro

Montage: Young Kobe alongside Shaq, followed by a mature Kobe guiding younger players like a sage.

Narrator: "From a talented rookie to the team's North Star, Kobe's journey was not just of skill refinement, but role evolution."

Lamar Odom (Ex-teammate): "Early on, Kobe was the prodigious student. But as time went, he became the teacher. He recognized what the team needed from him at every phase."

The Mamba Blueprint: Crafting a Legacy Amidst Dynamics

1. **Building Bonds Beyond the Court:**
   Clip: Kobe and teammates at a charity event, sharing laughter.
   Narrator: "It wasn't just about basketball. Kobe believed in connections, in knowing the person behind the jersey."
2. **Open Conversations, The Laker Way:**
   Footage: Team meetings where players speak passionately, Kobe listening intently.
   Narrator: "Creating a space where every voice mattered. That was Kobe's Laker way. And in those open forums, strategies were forged, and differences dissolved."
3. **Mentorship, The Mamba's Gift:**
   Clip: Kobe, in his later years, guiding younger players during practice.
   Narrator: "For Kobe, the gift of wisdom was to be passed down. His mentorship sculpted the next generation."

Ron Metta (Ex-teammate): "Man, he didn't just play with you. He grew with you. That's leadership."

Epilogue: Beyond the Trophies

Narrator: "Five NBA Championships, Olympic Gold, countless accolades. Yet, the resonance of Kobe Bryant's legacy is as much in the unseen – the huddles, the locker room conversations, the silent nods of understanding."

Fade out: An empty Lakers' court, the echo of a bouncing ball fading, symbolizing the everlasting impact of the Mamba and his mastery of team dynamics.

Narrator (softly): "In the heart of the City of Angels, amidst the bright lights and roaring crowds, the real magic was in the unity. The Symphony of the Mamba."

Scenario 10

Topic: Blockchain technology

Avatar: A beginner who knows nothing about blockchain.

Purpose and tone of the content written in what way: Simple and informative for beginners to understand complex ideas.

Prompt #1:

*Identify the top **6** authorities on **Blockchain technology** and give me their top **6** commonly shared facts and insights about **Blockchain technology**. Provide it in a list.*

Prompt #2:

Do you see any similarities and overlaps in the advice advocated from one authority to the next? Provide them all in a list.

Prompt #3:

*For the point **Potential Beyond Cryptocurrency** above, in the context of **Blockchain technology**:*

1. *Give a concise explanation of what it is*
2. *Explain the benefits and why it's beneficial*

3. *Describe the 3 most important aspects, why they are the most important aspects of that strategy, the role of each important aspect, the process of each important aspect, the benefit of each important aspect, how each important aspect can help you achieve or implement the point*
4. *Specify 3 practical pieces of advice or tips on what action to take*
5. *Specify 3 practical action steps*
6. *What likely outcome(s) might there be from taking the action in the context of **Blockchain technology**?*
7. *The key takeaway from this point.*

Prompt #4:

*For the point and aspects of **Potential Beyond Cryptocurrency** explained above, in terms of **Blockchain technology**: Generate a comprehensive and detailed chapter. Illustrate and explain the point and aspects of that point with examples and/or anecdotes that make it more relatable to **A beginner who knows nothing about blockchain**. Write it in a **Simple and informative way for beginners to understand complex ideas**. Use all the information provided for this point and aspects of this point in the previous responses to create in-depth and informative content.*

ChatGPT-4 final response:

 Chapter 5: Unveiling the Potential Beyond Cryptocurrency: How Blockchain Is Changing the World

Welcome to the future, where technology promises to revolutionize industries in ways we might not yet imagine. One such technology, blockchain, initially captured global attention through cryptocurrencies like Bitcoin. But as we delve deeper, we'll discover its profound potential beyond just digital money. So, let's embark on a journey to uncover the wonders of blockchain for a beginner.

Understanding Blockchain: The Simpler Side of a Complex Technology

Imagine a book where you write down every single transaction you've ever made in your life. Once written, it can't be changed or erased, and copies of this book are shared with a group of trusted friends for verification. Each new page (or set of transactions) is added with the consensus of your friends. This 'book' is akin to blockchain—a digital, transparent, tamper-proof, and decentralized ledger.

Why Blockchain is More Than Just Digital Coins

You might wonder, "What's so special about a digital book?" Well, beyond keeping track of digital coins, this unique 'book' can transform entire industries by providing trust, security, and efficiency.

For example, consider buying a house—an often complicated process with paperwork, agents, and intermediaries. With blockchain, the property's entire history could be available at your fingertips, from its original construction to the latest paint job. Secure, transparent, and without a mound of paperwork.

The Pillars of Blockchain Beyond Cryptocurrency:

1. **Decentralization: The Power of Collective Verification**
   * **What It Means:** Think of decentralization as a class project where every student checks each other's work instead of just the teacher doing it. No single student (or entity) has total control.
   * **Real-world Application:** Music streaming services like Spotify have sometimes been

criticized for not compensating artists fairly. Imagine a decentralized platform where artists upload their songs, and every time you listen, a small fee goes directly to them, without any middlemen taking a cut. This democratic and direct approach is enabled by the blockchain.

2. **Smart Contracts: Automation With Integrity**
   * **What It Means:** Imagine setting up a piggy bank that automatically releases money to your friend once you both run 5 miles, as recorded on your fitness apps. This self-executing contract is a basic example of a 'smart contract.'
   * **Real-world Application:** Let's say you order a custom-made watch. Instead of waiting, uncertain if it will arrive, a smart contract could be set up: once the tracking system confirms the delivery of the watch to your address, the payment is released to the seller. This ensures you get your item, and the seller gets their money, building trust without a need for intermediaries.

3. **Transparency with Privacy: Seeing Without Prying**

   * **What It Means:** It's like having a glass bank locker. Everyone can see there's something inside, but only you know its exact contents and value.
   * **Real-world Application:** Patient medical records are sensitive. With blockchain, a patient's health history can be transparently available to any doctor they visit, but the specifics can only be accessed with the patient's permission. This ensures seamless healthcare while safeguarding personal information.

Tips for Embracing Blockchain's Potential:

1. **Identify Needs First:** Before diving into blockchain solutions, understand what issues or inefficiencies you hope to address in your sector.

2. **Education is Power:** Equip yourself and your team with knowledge about blockchain. There are numerous online courses, workshops, and resources designed for beginners.
3. **Collaborate with Experts:** Don't go at it alone. Engage with blockchain experts to ensure the best practices are implemented for your specific needs.

Getting Started: Steps to Take Today

1. **Analyze and Assess:** Examine areas in your industry or life where transparency, security, and efficiency can be improved.
2. **Prototype and Pilot:** Before a full-fledged implementation, test the waters with a small project or a prototype to understand the technology's practical aspects.
3. **Feedback and Fine-tune:** Gather feedback from stakeholders and refine your approach. Remember, every new technology has a learning curve.

The Future Awaits

The potential outcomes of integrating blockchain are immense. From establishing trust in systems and achieving significant cost reductions to enhanced security against fraud, the benefits are game-changing.

Key Takeaway: Blockchain is not just about digital coins. It's a revolutionary technology that promises to reshape industries, offering transparency, security, and efficiency. As you move forward in your blockchain journey, remember that it's about building trust, simplifying complex processes, and envisioning a more connected, transparent world.

With this knowledge, you're now equipped to explore and possibly implement blockchain in areas beyond just cryptocurrency. Welcome to the future!

Conclusion

These prompt templates, together with ChatGPT, save time during the research, outline, and draft phases of creating content. It also helps you to structure and tone the content for your intended audience.

Allowing ChatGPT to assist in certain aspects of creating content that can take days, weeks, or even months saves time. You can direct your focus and effort on other aspects of creating content and what ChatGPT cannot do.

You may find that not only does your production increase, but also the quality of your work.

The more you use these prompt templates in different scenarios, the easier and more natural it will become.

In the first few weeks of incorporating these prompt templates, I was constantly buzzing with ideas and new scenarios to test and making notes everywhere. While you were reading, I'm sure you had quite a few of your own.

Put those ideas into the prompt templates, and 10 minutes from now, you could have a rough draft on your hands.

Final note: If I haven't made it clear, ChatGPT is best used as a tool and assistant to help you with everything from grammar to idea generation, research to tone. Don't use the responses from it as is. Check your work in a tool like Originality.ai to see the A.I. Content Score of your content. Algorithms can detect if an A.I. produced content. Just. Don't. Do. It.

Thanks for reading, and I sincerely hope this book helps your writing process!

Review Request

Most of us don't spend time reviewing items we like. We only write reviews when we are dissatisfied. Usually, we don't review what we enjoy and only review things when we are unhappy. However, the best way to get more good products out there is to let people know you are satisfied with them.

You may underestimate how valuable even a short review is to an author. Most of us read every single review. It also helps us improve our writing, message, and how we serve you.

If you found this book helpful, and I sincerely hope you did, please leave me an honest review on Amazon.

Thank you.

Made in the USA
Monee, IL
01 December 2023

47948521R00044